MACHINERY OF THE MIND

Dion Fortune ™

S.I.L (Trading) Ltd
London

The Machinery of The Mind by Violet M. Firth.
With a foreword by A. G. Tansley. F.R.S.

Violet M. Firth adopted the nom de plume Dion Fotune for
most of her works.

CONTENTS

First published 1922 by George Allen & Unwin
This edition published 1995 by SIL Trading Ltd.

ISBN 1 899585 00 1

© Society of the Inner Light 1995

A CIP catalogue record for this book is available from the
British Library.

Typeset and Design by Clinton Smith Design Consultants,
London.

Printed and bound in Great Britain.

PREFACE

The works of the late Dion Fortune were written a long time ago and since then a great deal more has been understood and realised so that many of the ideas then expressed are not now necessarily acceptable.

Psychism is simply one type of of inner awareness and there are other types at least as valid and as common. Non-psychic readers, therefore, can translate experience in terms of psychic imagery into terms of their inner awareness.

The publication of these books continues because there is still much value in them and because they can act as valuable pointers to seekers.

Details of the aims and work of the Society of the Inner Light, founded by Dion Fortune, may be obtained by writing (with postage please) to the Secretariat at 38 Steele's Road, London NW3 4RG, England.

FOREWORD

I am very glad to have the opportunity of commending this little volume to those without any previous knowledge who desire to gain a clear idea of the way in which modern psychology regards the human mind.

For every time the words 'psychology' and 'psychological' were used in the newspapers ten years ago, they must be used fifty times today; and though very often some other word would do just as well, or, a good deal better, this sudden vogue has a real meaning. The public has become aware of the existence of psychology: people are beginning to realise that the human mind, the instrument by which we know and think and feel and strive, must itself be studied for its own sake if we are to gain a deeper understanding and a greater control of human life.

A distinct reaction from the rather narrow materialism of the end of the nineteenth and the beginning of the twentieth centuries, an increased realisation of immaterial or 'spiritual' values has helped towards giving the mind its rightful place in human interest. On the one hand, modern academic psychology has for many years now been gradually emancipating itself from the chaotic subjectivities of competing philosophies, and developing on really scientific lines, with the aid of accurate observation, comparison and experiment. Its genuinely and increasingly useful applications to education and to industry are evidences of that.

On the other hand, the remarkable results of psychoanalysis have been made widely known, though often with that misleading one-sided emphasis which seemed fated to attend the popularisation of any branch of scientific enquiry. And these results have been found not only interesting but exciting - to some morbidly exciting - because they appeal to instincts and emotions which our civilisation represses and often perverts. Psychoanalysis has indeed become a fashionable craze, and as such has doubtless done a certain amount of harm and has met with a good deal of opprobrium from the serious-minded. But psychoanalysis has come to stay, because, however much it may be misused by the ignorant, the unbalanced and the half-educated, it is both a sound technique of research and a sound therapeutic method. And it certainly has a most important contribution to make to the psychology of the future.

This little book, which can be read through at a sitting, succeeds in the difficult task of presenting the rudiments of the modern view of the mind in an easy, lucid and attractive form. Though I may not agree with every sentence she has written, Miss Firth's development of the subject, and of its very intimate connection with human life and human troubles, seems to me not only substantially sound and accurate, but essentially sane and well balanced. Her explanation of the different levels of the mind and of the 'censors' by the metaphor of the tank and the sieves is particularly ingenious and helpful. The book will certainly succeed, to use the author's words, in planting certain fundamental concepts in untrained minds so that they may serve as a basis for future studies.

A. G. TANSLEY.

INTRODUCTION

Originally given as a popular lecture course, this little book does not pretend to be a contribution to the formidable array of psychological literature. It is intended for those who have neither the time nor the training necessary to assimilate the standard works on the subject, but who want to know its elements; and to understand the principles on which our characters are formed and the means by which the process of thought is carried on, not so much from the scholastic point of view, as in relation to the problems of everyday life.

It is hoped that many will find herein the key to things that have puzzled them in their own natures, for only those who hold such unsolved problems in their hearts can know how crippling and tormenting they are.

This book does not aim so much at an orderly setting forth of the elements of psychology as at planting certain fundamental concepts in untrained minds so that they may serve as a basis for future studies. To this end the writer has adopted a pictorial, almost diagrammatic method of presentation in order that a framework of general ideas may be formed into which details may subsequently be fitted, having found this to be the best way to convey novel concepts to minds untrained in metaphysical subtleties.

The teachings of no special school of psychology are adhered to; the writer is indebted to all, but loyal to none, holding that in the absence of any accepted standard of authority in psychological science each student must review the doctrines offered for his adherence in the light of his own experience.

This book is essentially practical in aim, written in response to a practical need. In her experience of remedial psychology, the writer saw that many cases of mental and nervous trouble would never have developed if their victims had had an elementary knowledge of the workings of the mind; she also found that many patients required nothing but an explanation of these principles to put them on the road to recovery, and that even when more than this was needed to effect a cure, such a knowledge greatly expedited the treatment by enabling the patient to co-operate intelligently.

So far as she is aware, there is no book that deals with psychopathology, not from the point of view of the student, but from that of the patient who needs an elementary knowledge of the laws of the mind in order to enable him to think hygienically. This book is written to fulfil that need; it is not only applicable, however, to those who are sick in mind or estate, but to those also who desire to develop their latent capacities by means of the practical application of the laws of thought and character.

1
THE PHYSICAL VEHICLE
OF CONSCIOUSNESS

In order to arrive at an adequate understanding of mental processes it is necessary to have some idea of the machinery whereby the mind makes contact with the body.

Throughout every inch of our organism is a network of specialised fibres whose function it is to carry nervous impulses from the sense organs to the central nervous system of brain and spinal cord, and from thence out again to the muscles, glands, and other organs of reaction. The sense organs act as receivers of sensation, the nerve fibres as transmitters, the central nervous system as a general telephone exchange, and the muscles, glands, and organs as the executants of the impulses of the mind.

Sense organs consist of cells, or sets of cells, specialised for the reception of particular kinds of impressions. That is to say, if the particular kind of stimulus they are fitted to receive is, administered to them, a change, probably of a chemical type, takes place in their substance, which, it is thought, gives rise to energy of an electrical nature, which runs along the nerve fibre as along a wire. At the present moment, however, our knowledge of the nature of the nervous impulse is tentative and hypothetical.

Like all other living tissue, the nervous system is built up of millions of specialised cells. These cells consist of a main cell body with prolongations, usually two in number. One of these has a mass of branching fibres like the root of a plant, and is called the DENDRON; the other consists of a long thread, the end of which is frayed out into strand as the end of a piece of worsted may be unravelled. This process is called the AXON.

The thread-like branches of the axon of one cell interlace with these of the dendron of another cell, and a nervous impulse, running down the nerve fibres, jumps the gap in the same way as the electric current jumps the space between the terminals of an arc lamp.

It will readily be seen that these interlacing fibrils, millions in number, ramifying throughout every portion of the body, form a most wonderful system of communication; the brain and spinal cord acting as a central telephone exchange.

Muscles are composed of long, spindle-shaped cells which are capable of contraction. Chemical changes are constantly going on in their substance. The blood and lymph which bathe them bring food materials and carry away the waste products of their activity.

These food substances, which are highly organised chemical compounds, are stored in the body of the cell. When a nervous impulse is received, these food globules, as it were, explode; that is to say, they break down into their component chemical parts, and the energy which went to build them up is set free in the process and performs the work for which the muscle is designed.

The glands are the chemists of the body, and in the crucibles of their minute cells carry out the wonderful processes of living chemistry upon which our vital functions are based. The quantity and quality of their output is controlled by the nervous system, which acts as regulator of every process of the body.

2
THE EVOLUTION OF
THE NERVOUS SYSTEM

The easiest way to grasp the organisation of our complex nervous structure is to study its evolution from its humble beginnings in the simplest forms of life.

In single-celled animalacula, the most primitive type of living creatures, a single cell performs all the functions of life; it moves, breathes, assimilates, excretes, and feels. With the development of multicellular organisms, however, different cells are given different work to do, and made to do that, and nothing else.

It then becomes necessary that coordination should be maintained between the sense organs that perceive the prey and the muscles that move to its capture, and for this purpose other cells are told off to specialise in communication.

Thus it will be seen that the functional unit of the nervous system is not the nerve cell, but what is called the SENSORI-MOTOR ARC, consisting of a nerve carrying the incoming sensation from a sense organ and making contact with another nerve which carries the outgoing impulse to a muscle or organ.

When a multiplicity of muscles becomes available for movement, it is necessary to further link up the sensori-motor arcs, so that other parts of the structure may be brought into play, and the response not be confined to one muscle alone; so nerve cells form loops upon the arcs, and loops upon the loops, with further intercommunications among themselves, the organisation becoming more and more elaborate, admitting of more and more complex reactions to stimulus, till finally the wonderful complications of the human brain are achieved.

3
HOW AN IDEA ENTERS THE MIND

When an impression is made on a sense organ, the sensation derived from it is telegraphed up the connecting nerve fibre to the brain, and there translated, by a process of which we know nothing, from a sensation to a thought.

We believe that the mind learns by experience to associate certain kinds of sensation with certain objects or conditions in the environment, and when it feels these particular sensations, deduces that certain objects are present, and forms mental images, or thought models intended to represent these objects.

The truth of our precepts is determined by the closeness with which our thought model corresponds to its original. An exact copy is a true concept, an imperfect copy an inaccurate concept.

We 'recognise' an object by a process of classification, noting its likeness or unlikeness to other objects already known. When an unfamiliar object attracts our attention, we put it through a process of comparison until we find to which compartment in our concept-pictures it should be assigned, and if we cannot find a perfect match, we put it in the most suitable compartment we can discover, and then partition off a little subclass for it, thus admitting its identity in essentials, but its difference in details from the other occupants of that compartment.

For example, supposing we were to land on an island and an object on the shore attracted our attention, we should try to see what class of things of which we already had experience it most closely resembled. We should observe its movements, and assign it to the class of living creatures; see its four limbs

15

and hair, and conclude it was an animal. Note its upright attitude, clothes, and weapons, and recognise these as characteristic of humanity; but perceiving that its skin differed in colour from that of any human being we had ever seen before, we should partition off a fresh subdivision in the department of our mind in which our ideas connected with humanity were stored, place it there, and probably give it a distinguishing name by means of which we could indicate it to other human beings.

Supposing, however, we presently come across another object of the same nature, we should not have to make a fresh subdivision for it, but would classify it with the previously examined specimen, and thus we should feel this time that we 'knew what it was'. In fact, the process of 'knowing' is a process of classification, and we feel that we 'know' a thing when we have assigned it to a satisfactory pigeon-hole among our concepts.

4
THE ORGANISATION OF THE
UPPER LEVELS OF THE MIND

Those untrained in psychology generally conceive of the mind as a homogeneous whole; our first systematic examination reveals to us, however, that the mind is just as organic as the body.

The organisation of the mind may best be realised by thinking of it as a tank across which, at different heights, are placed sieves of varying coarseness of mesh. We must conceive of the mind as being composed of certain layers, and the layer in which our conscious life has its most permanent focus we will consider to be the outermost layer and name THE FOCUS OF CONSCIOUSNESS. Immediately behind the Focus of Consciousness lies the level which psychologists call THE FRINGE OF CONSCIOUSNESS, and the two are divided from one another by a sieve-like mechanism which is technically called a CENSOR.

The understanding of these two levels of the mind may be rendered clearer if we next consider the uses to which they are put. Supposing a person is sitting in a room listening to a lecture, of what will he be aware? Firstly, his attention will be concentrated upon the lecture, and, secondly, he will be dimly conscious of the sounds made by the traffic in the street outside. By an effort of will he will pay attention to those ideas only which are connected with the lecture, and exclude from consciousness those which are connected with the street traffic; or, to express the process in psychological terms, we may say that all the ideas connected with the lecture are admitted to the focus of consciousness and all ideas connected with the street noises are kept in the fringe of consciousness, and that the censor-sieve is so adjusted that ideas in the fringe may not intrude upon the focus. Its meshes may be conceived as being of such a size that only the compact little ideas appertaining to the lecture can pass through them, and the undefined ideas connected with the street traffic are held back.

It will readily be seen that our powers of concentration depend upon the satisfactory fructfifying of this psychic sieve. The more we can bring the adjustment of its meshes under voluntary control, the better will be our powers of concentration; whereas, if its mesh be loose or faulty, and we have acquired little or no control over it, we shall find that we are unable to hold our mind to any consecutive train of thought, and that our focus of consciousness is constantly liable to be invaded by ideas alien to the matter to which we wish to pay attention.

These two levels, the Focus and FRINGE OF CONSCIOUS-NESS, together comprise what is known as THE CONSCIOUS MIND. This is the part of the mind which most truly seems to be 'our-self'. It is the section of the mind in which we carry on all our conscious mental activities, but it is by no means the whole of the mental house.

Immediately behind the fringe of consciousness comes the level of the mind which is known as the FORECONSCIOUS, PRECONSCIOUS, and many other things according to the school of psychology whose doctrines are adhered to. If, however, its function be understood, it will be readily enough recognised through the disguise of the varied nomenclature which, unfortunately, complicates the study of psychology.

In this level of the mind are stored all the ideas which we hold in memory, but are not actually thinking about. It may, in fact, be defined as the level of conscious memory, and just as the focus is separated from the fringe of consciousness by an adjustable censor-sieve, so an exactly similar sieve interposes between the fringe of consciousness and the foreconscious, and works upon exactly the same principles.

Thus, the student listening to the lecture could adjust this second sieve so as to allow everything he had ever learnt that had any bearing upon the subject in hand, to rise into the focus of consciousness and help him to understand the lecture. It is this faculty which is of such great importance in determining the critical powers of the mind, for the previously determined ideas, ranging themselves alongside the fresh concepts offered for assimilation, serve as standards of value, and form a running commentary upon the lecture.

These three levels together, the focus, the fringe, and the foreconscious, form the level of the mind to which we have access and of which we can make use; but we must note this point in connection with these levels, that any idea which we may wish to consider must be placed in the strong light of the focus of consciousness before we can see it clearly; we cannot consider an idea while it is still in the foreconscious, but we can, at will, take it out of the foreconscious and place it in the focus of consciousness for our consideration.

Indeed, these three levels of the mind may be likened to a kitchen, the foreconscious being the cupboard, the fringe of consciousness the table, and the focus of consciousness the mixing basin; and the ideas upon the three levels may be represented by the ingredients of the pudding, some of which are put away in the cupboard, some lie ready to the hand upon the table, and others are actually in the mixing basin being stirred.

Those on the table, like the ideas in the fringe of consciousness, lie ready to the cook's hand, but she is not dealing with them at the moment; those in the cupboard (the foreconscious) are out of sight, but she knows they are there and can get them if she wants them; but it is only those that are in the basin, the focus of consciousness, that she is actually at work upon.

To the average man these three levels constitute all there is of his mind, he has no conception of the strange hinterland lying behind the narrow strip of civilised coast, yet it is here that the springs of his being take their rise, and it is the discovery and exploration of this hinterland which has been the great contribution of modern psychology to the sum of human knowledge.

5
THE ORGANISATION OF
THE LOWER LEVELS OF THE MIND

In the level of the mind known as the subconscious or unconscious are stored all the ideas to which we have no direct
access.

Some psychologists say that the memory of every impression
which has ever been received by a sense organ is registered
here as on a photographic plate, but this opinion is not
universally accepted. We shall be quite safe in saying, however, that the memory of anything which has ever made a
distinct impression on the mind is stored here and plays its
part in the mental life.

Between the subconscious and the foreconscious is placed the
great main censor-sieve of the mind, and it is this which is
meant when the 'censor' is referred to in psychoanalytical
literature.

This censor-sieve is of the greatest importance in the mental
economy, for upon its function the health of the mind is
largely dependant. If its meshes are too loose, we get an
uprush into consciousness of ideas which should never be
there; and if too tight, the conscious mind is cut off from the
source of its energy, the subconscious.

This sieve is constructed upon the same principles as the two
others which we have already considered, but it has one
fundamental difference, it is not under the control of the will;
the dimension of its mesh is regulated, not by what I, at the
moment, may happen to wish, but by what the main tenor of
my character may determine.

The foreconscious, then, may be likened to a reference library,
but the great storehouse of the subconscious is a vault in

21

which the archives are kept; and although the bulk of them never touch the conscious mind, it is their indirect influence which determines the tone of the character.

The remotest level of the mind, whose functioning is purely automatic, has the control of all the vital functions of the body. Its thought processes direct the activities of the spinal level of the nervous system, whereas the other levels of the mind have the brain as their physical organ of manifestation, as is proved by the fact that a disease of the brain can throw the reasoning faculties out of gear and leave the purely physiological nervous functions intact, whereas a disease of the spinal cord may render inoperative the nervous processes of the bodily functions, though the mental processes are unimpaired.

The psychic processes of the automatic mind govern all the biochemical processes of the body; it is this level which controls the involuntary muscles, regulates the blood supply to any part of the body, controls the output of the ductless glands, and hence the chemical composition of the blood. It is these facts which may throw light upon the origin of many functional disturbances and upon the phenomena of mental healing.

Although the automatic level is not normally in touch with the conscious mind, it is enormously affected by the general feeling-tone of the mentality, and especially by the emotional states of the subconscious, hence the alterations of physiological function which take place in nervous disease.

This level of the mind was the first to be organised in the history of biological development. The dim mentation of the rudimentary beginnings of life was of the automatic order, being entirely concerned with physiological processes.

As organisms became more evolved, a higher type of intelligence was necessary for the carrying out of their life activities, and we get mentation of the type that is carried on in the subconscious level, the impulsive mentation of the instincts.

Level by level the mind builds itself up, in the race and in the individual; and level by level, under the influence of old age, disease or drugs, the planes of consciousness break down in the inverse order to that in which they developed, the more recently organised higher centres going first, and the automatic mind, the oldest and most stable, with aeons of habit behind it, working on to the last, keeping the bodily mechanism running long after all that made the organism a man has withdrawn from its dishonoured vehicle.

6
COMPLEXES

Having studied the levels into which the mind is divided, we must next consider the nature of the material that is stored in them, and to do this we must study the workings of MEMORY.

When an idea enters the mind it does not remain an independent unit for very long. It seems to be a fundamental characteristic of ideas that they form alliances among themselves, and these groups of ideas are technically known as COMPLEXES.

A complex may be compared to the branching growth of a pond weed; it has a central starting point from which ramify threads that divide and subdivide, and branch in every direction, and connect it with other systems of ideas that have similar branching threads. Thus it is that if an idea on any subject enters our consciousness, we find that it is not an isolated unit, but one end of a chain which branches into all sorts of side issues; we have not touched a single line of thought, but a whole railway system.

These systems of ideas spread and ramify through all the levels of the mind, but if we trace them far enough, we shall invariably find that they have their roots in one of the great primal instincts, deep down in the subconscious. It is from this that they derive the vitality that binds them together, for all complexes have a core of emotion, and it is from the instincts that the emotions spring.Let us take an example from actual life, and see how these principles work. A man may, for example, be a grocer - he will therefore have a Grocery Complex, that is to say, all his ideas connected with the buying and selling of household commodities will be linked together, so that if a train of thought be started in connection with any one aspect of his business, by an easy transition many other aspects may drift into his mind.

Now, grocery is not in itself an absorbing subject, like literature or science, yet the man is interested in it; and why? Because his grocery complex has its root in his self-preservation instinct, for it is the means by which he keeps himself alive. If his grocery business prospers, he feels pleasure, because it means a fuller and pleasanter life for him; if it diminishes, he feels pain and fear, because his means of keeping himself alive are threatened.

In addition to being a grocer, however, he may be an elder of the local chapel, and have a far-reaching complex of religious interests, ramifying, interlacing, and having their instinctive roots in his subconscious, just as his grocery complex has. Then, one day, he may be looking up the current price of pepper in his trade list, and from pepper his thoughts pass to spices in general; their pungent odour suggests incense, and he asks himself whether ritualism is ever allowable. It will here be seen that a trailing branch of his grocery complex has made contact with his religious complex and brought it into consciousness.

Again, our grocer may be thinking of getting married, and immediately his grocery complex throws out a side shoot which strikes root in his reproductive instinct, and his interest in grocery is reinforced by much of the interest which gathers round sex in his life, for it is upon the prosperity of his business that his prospect of marriage depends.

Thus it will be seen that the mind is filled with a ramifying mass of complexes which throw out branches in every direction, and that if the end of any thread be caught hold of, by gently pulling upon it we can draw all the complexes with which it is connected into consciousness. This is how memory works, and even if an idea has been 'forgotten', that is, passed from the conscious into the subconscious, it is still possible to recover it by taking advantage of this tendency of ideas to stick together; for by gently pulling upon the parts of the complex to which it is affiliated which are in consciousness, the branchings which are in the subconscious can be coaxed into light. It is upon this factor that psychoanalysis bases much of its work.

Ideas tend to group themselves in complexes according to certain well-defined principles.

I.   Any ideas connected with the same subject tend to become associated together.

II. Ideas which enter the mind at the same time tend to become associated together. For instance, if I have a nasty fall on a piece of banana skin while going to the pillar-box, when I see bananas I shall think of falls and pillar-boxes, and when I see pillar-boxes, I may think of bananas and falls.

III. Ideas of cause and effect become associated together.

IV. Ideas which have any sort of resemblance, fundamental or superficial, tend to recall one another. Thus, if I think of sausages, I may be put in mind of Zeppelins, and if I think of the fall on the banana skin, my mind may leap to the Niagara Falls or fallen women.

This irrational method of thought is of enormous importance in applied psychology, for much of the thinking carried on by the subconscious mind is done in this way, and it gives rise to that peculiar method of thought which will be dealt with in the chapter on symbolism.

7
THE INSTINCTS

We have already considered the mind as a tank divided into compartments by sieves of varying diameters of mesh, let us now consider the currents that move in the water that fills the tank. We may diagrammatically conceive the inflow as taking place through one main channel into the subconscious, and there dividing into three streams. This main channel of energy, which supplies the motive power of all living creatures, has been called by many names: libido, horme, elan vitale, and bio-urge; an adequate English equivalent is the thrust of life.

This stream of psychic energy becomes specialised in the individual into divergent currents, which we call the three great instincts. The first of these is the SELF-PRESERVA-TION INSTINCT. Under this heading may be gathered up all the activities which are motived by (1) the Will to Live, or Self-Maintenance, and, (2) the Will to Live more Fully, or Self-Aggrandisement.

The second great instinct is that OF REPRODUCTION, or sex, whose function it is to secure race preservation. Through this channel tends to go the surplus of energy left over after the demands of self-maintenance have been fulfiled.

The third great instinct is the SOCIAL or HERD INSTINCT, by which term we designate that system of innate tendencies and capacities which enables us to cooperate with our fellows and lead a social life, with all its advantages and disadvantages.
Some animals, however, do not have this third instinct, but lead solitary lives, acknowledging no ties save those of mate and offspring; but the more highly evolved types, including man, have developed this great specialisation of psychic ener-

gy which enables them to lead a social life.

These three great instincts act and react on each other in the hidden field of the subconscious, and build up social organisation and individual character.

In order to understand the workings of the instincts, however, it must be clearly realised that they are universal and not personal in their scope; the survival or suffering of the unit are not considered in the scheme of things, it is the race that counts.

If we regard the instincts as subserving the welfare of the individual only, we form a concept which cannot fail to lead us astray when we seek to put our conclusions to a practical application. The workings of instinct must be viewed from the standpoint of evolutionary progress, not individual well-being. This is the point of view from which Nature frames her schemes, and we can only hope to understand her ways if we occupy her standpoint.

To regard man as actuated by reason is a hopeless error. Instinct forms the mainspring of his action, and reason is used to carry out the promptings of instinct. It must be remembered, however, that instinct does not function in crude physical forms only. Man possesses emotions and intellect as well as a body, and upon each plane of his being the instincts express themselves appropriately, functioning emotionally and intellectually as well as physically. A man uses his wits as well as his muscles in the struggle for self-preservation, and the sex instinct is not exhausted by the physical act of procreation.

Emphasis is laid upon this point, because herein lies the key to the practical application of psychology to human life.

The emotions have their sources in the instincts indeed, an emotion may be said to be the subjective aspect of an instinct. If an instinct is achieving its aim, we feel pleasure - if it is being frustrated, we feel pain - and if we anticipate its frustration, we feel fear.

Whenever there is emotion, some underlying instinct must have been stirred into activity. It will thus be seen how predominating is the influence exerted by the instincts upon our lives; they may, in fact, be considered the mainsprings of motive.

At one time psychology busied itself with the reasoning processes, and looked upon man as a rational being, and indeed the man in the street still considers himself as such, but the researches of modern psychology have shown us that emotion and not reason is the actuating force, and that reason is a tool in the service of the emotions.

8
THE SELF-PRESERVATION INSTINCT

The self-preservation instinct appears to our consciousness under the guise of that deep-rooted clinging to life, that desire to live, which characterises every living thing. It is this instinct, functioning simply in simply organised creatures, that leads them to seek food and avoid danger, and also causes that complex organism, a civilised man, to carry out the elaborate activities of 'earning a living'.

It is essentially a selfish instinct, for it leads the individual to regard his own welfare alone, and to consider others only so far as their existence is essential to his. For instance, shooting and hunting during the breeding season are forbidden by law, not out of consideration for the hunted creatures, but because the continuation of their species is useful to us.

Its influence, however, is often modified by the two other great instincts whose influence may become so strong under certain circumstances as to induce a man not only to disregard his own interests, but even to lay down his life for others.

In many varieties of animals, however, only two instincts are present, self preservation and reproduction - but in animals that are associated together into herds or packs, a third instinct is developed, the social instinct. When this occurs, the functioning of the self-preservation instinct is greatly modified; the individual no longer owes his existence solely to his power to cope with his environment, but depends mainly upon his ability to keep his place in the herd; and

upon the social organisation devolves the task of adaptation and survival. The strayed sheep is soon hunted down, the solitary wolf starves.

This is equally true of man, who is also a social animal. The misery of Central Europe, in the breakdown of social organisation following upon the war, has shown us the helplessness of the individual human being and his complete dependence upon herd life.

The self-preservation instinct and its ruthless functioning under the law of natural selection has furnished a theme to many moralists and sociologists of the materialistic type, but they are apt to forget that the socialisation of humanity has changed the nature of the problem; the unit of survival is no longer the individual, but the social organisation of which he is a member. The law of self preservation has given place to the law of group preservation, and the centre of psychic gravity is shifted. The importance of this point cannot be over-estimated in practical psychology.

By some psychologists the instinct of nutrition is distinguished from that of self preservation, but for all practical purposes they are identical.

It must be born in mind, in applying the standards of psychology to the human character, that in the more highly developed types of human being the self-preservation instinct is not fulfiled simply by the continuance of physical life; there is self preservation of the personality as well as of the bodily existence, and unless a man has adequate scope for self expression and self development, he will experience that sense of incompleteness and imperfection characteristic of the repression of an instinct.

9
DISEASES OF THE
SELF-PRESERVATION INSTINCT

The self-preservation instinct, having its source in the sense of individuality, of separateness, is the motive of our self assertion. It is necessary that each member of a herd should have a certain amount of self assertiveness in order to maintain his place among his fellows. If, however, this quality is above or below the requisite standard, his survival will be endangered; if, on the one hand, he is lacking in self assertion, he will not obtain his fair share of the means of life available for the group of which he is a member. On the other hand, if his self assertion is excessive, it may disrupt the social organisation, and either lead to the extinction of the group, or to his ejection from it. Lack of self-preservation instinct is usually due to deep-seated psycho-pathologies, too complex to be entered upon here - but we may say in passing that this failure is often due to a division of aims in the subconscious mind, the individual is not sure which self he ought to preserve, and so preserves neither.

An excess of self preservation is often developed in the child who has had a hard struggle to find and express his individuality.

The self-preservation instinct has a great influence upon vitality. All observant persons must have noticed how easily the man who has lost his hold upon life, or has given up hope, succumbs to disease.

10
THE REPRODUCTIVE INSTINCT

The reproductive instinct is Nature's mechanism for ensuring the continuation of the species, and its subjective aspect appears to us as all the emotions and sensations connected with sex.

As soon as the demands of the self-preservation instinct are satisfied, as soon as the individual is secure, adequately fed and sufficiently developed, then life tends to overflow the vessel it has filled, and this psychic pressure constitutes sex desire.

Sex, however, must not be considered under its physical manifestations only, it has an emotional and mental aspect as well. It is more than the mere overflow of energy in the act of procreation, it is also the desire for the rejuvenation and vital stimulus that is produced by the act of union. Whosoever in considering human problems fails to look beyond the physical stratum of the sex instinct, cannot fail to obtain a false perspective.

It has been laid down as a maxim that psychology and physiology ought to be kept strictly separate, but it is impossible to treat adequately of the sex instinct without considering it under both its aspects, for sex activity works in a psycho-physical circle; organic sensations stimulate the emotions, and the emotions react on the organs. A sexual image rising in the mind brings about the preliminary reaction of the physical organs of its expression; and any irritation of the physical organs, however accidental, tends to produce a corresponding emotional state. Stimulus may occur at any point on the psycho-physical circuit, and so may inhibition.
The sex instinct forms the nucleus of a huge complex, second only to the group of ideas that centres round the individual-

ity itself. To all ideas and activities that are in any way connected with the gratification of the sexual desire, its energy readily passes over. Dress, the home, the ambitions, each and all may owe their interest to the reproductive instinct which uses them as channels for its fulfilment.

11
DEVELOPMENT OF THE
REPRODUCTIVE INSTINCT

The sex instinct, in the course of development from its infantile aspect to its adult manifestation, goes through well-marked phases which are little known outside the ranks of the psychotherapists, but which are of great importance to the educationalist and sociologist.

The sexuality of the child is simply a capacity for deriving gratification from certain feelings, and it is a diffused and vague sensation that he experiences; this capacity, however, as the child grows older, becomes gradually concentrated upon its physiological channels of activity, and as it becomes concentrated it increases in intensity, just as the placid waters of a broad and shallow river become deep and headlong in a ravine.

The interests of a very young child only gradually extend beyond his own bodily sensations, and he therefore leads an existence that is self-centred beyond any adult conception of the term. The organs of reproduction, being very highly nerved in preparation for their future functions, are found to be capable of keener sensation than the rest of the body, and therefore attract his attention. This is the AUTO-EROTIC STAGE.

The, to a child, striking manifestations connected with the exercise of the bodily functions also attract his interest. This is the COPROPHILIC STAGE.

Later, his curiosity concerning his own body being satisfied, he begins to be curious concerning the bodies of others. This is called the HOMOSEXUAL STAGE, the stage wherein he is interested in bodies of the same sex as his own, but it might more truly be called the stage of undifferentiated interest, for the child is only interested in those who are made in the same way as himself, because he is not aware that anyone is made differently.

This curiosity being outgrown, his interest is transferred to those who are different from himself, regardless as to whether they are closely related to him or not. Soon, however, he begins to differentiate between his immediate relations and those who are less closely connected. This is called by psychologists 'the raising of the incest barriers', but to the child it appears simply as a moving on of the focus of interest; he is no longer attracted by his mother and sisters, not because he feels it is wrong to have such feelings towards them, but because familiarity breeds contempt, and gives rise to the state of mind that is expressed in the phrase 'insipid as sisters kisses'.

The child has now attained the adult attitude towards sex, and it only remains for the physical organs to make their corresponding development at the time of puberty for the circuit to be complete.

12
DISEASES OF THE REPRODUCTIVE INSTINCT

I. Should an individual be lacking in vigour, he may fail to reach his full psychic development, and stick fast at one of the earlier phases. The adult sex force therefore manifests itself in an immature form, and the individual is a pervert of a congenital type. Strange as it may seem, his peculiarity will appear to him as normal and natural, and will not interfere with the development of a high type of character and perfect health, though his path through life is rendered a difficult one owing to the insuperable obstacles to the satisfaction of his love nature.

Two courses are open to him. He may become an actual pervert, in which case he incurs the censure of society, because he is unfaithful to his trust in not using the overflow of his life force for the upbuilding of the herd, but expends it through channels that cannot lead to reproduction and thus wastes it; also because any sexual abnormality is exceedingly infectious, owing to the force of suggestion, whether by example or precept, and would lead other and normal individuals to similar antisocial action. It is this strong race-preservation instinct that gives rise to the disgust and anger of the normal individual at all forms of abnormality.

The unfortunate, however, may instead become a potential pervert, and repress into his subconscious mind desires which he feels to be wrong; he tries to lead a normal life, but the adult form of sex does not satisfy him, and in his heart he really desires the abnormal form which he should have outgrown and left behind. This wish, not being allowed by the censor to enter consciousness, has recourse to symbolic expression and gives rise to many forms of insanity and neuroticism.

37

II. An individual may be developing quite normally, when some shock, often quite slight, or some undue pressure of environment, may artificially arrest his development, and he will go through much the same phases as the potential pervert, but being of better mental material to begin with, he will usually incline towards neurotic disease rather than insanity.

Those who have the care of children should be careful not to give the child a shock by administering a severe reprimand when his curiosities and activities take an undesirable form; such action gives the matter undue prominence in the child's mind, and may lead to a stoppage of development at the phase represented by the undesirable activity. Explanation and counsel will be more effective than a scolding, and leave no undesirable after effects.

III. An individual may reach normal adulthood quite safely, but, his energies finding no outlet on that level owing to force of circumstances, they may revert to one of the primitive phases through which he has passed, and he may acquire a perversion of sexual habit with the same liabilities to disease that we have noted above.

IV. Excessive sexual activity may lead to jaded powers of response to normal sexual stimuli, and the individual may then deliberately turn to abnormal forms of gratification in the hope of obtaining satisfaction.

13
SUBLIMATION

Should an instinct be denied its expression and all ideas connected with it be repressed into the subconscious, trouble will ensue. The lower reaches of a river can be emptied by the simple expedient of placing a dam across its channel, but this does not solve the problem of the surplus water, which gathers head behind the obstruction till it bursts its banks and makes a morass of the upper reaches. If it is necessary to deflect a river from its bed, then an alternative course must be provided, for the water continues to come down from the hills and must by some means be disposed of.

It is precisely this engineering problem that the psychotherapist has to deal with. We know that a large percentage of mental and nervous disorders are caused by the repression of the sex instinct. This great instinct, in its mental and physical aspects, is so fundamental and so powerful that it cannot with safety to the individual be entirely repressed, nor with safety to society be given free rein, and we are on the horns of a dilemma, for social laws demand that it shall only be expressed under very limited conditions those of legal marriage and even then not to an unlimited extent; and nature demands that it shall be expressed as soon as the physical organs of its manifestation are sufficiently developed to function.

The average man solves this problem for himself by conniving at the maintenance of a pariah class of women whose very existence is socially ignored and is a fertile source of misery, disease, and crime; but for women, unless they are prepared permanently to join the pariah class, a social safety valve does not exist, and we find among them a much higher percentage than among men suffering from those nervous troubles that are due to a repression of the sex instinct, and this also applies to men who, whether from idealism or fear of disease, do not avail themselves of a compromise.

This problem would prove as intractable in the future as it has in the past were it not that we now know that the law of transmutation of energy from one form to another is as true for psychology as it is for physics, and sex force can be utilised for other purposes than physical reproduction. This process of conversion is technically known as SUBLIMATION.

This is one of the most important discoveries of modern psychology, for it provides the solution to grave social problems that menace the fabric of civilisation.

How, in actual practice, can this result be achieved?

First, by altering our entire attitude toward sex, and realising that a problem is not solved by ignoring its existence. Secondly, by taking the sex problem out of the domain of the subconscious into the conscious mind and frankly facing it, and acquiring dominion over it by the practice of thought control, transmuting our emotions instead of repressing them; and thirdly, by providing a channel of creative interest down which may flow the energies we wish to deflect from their primitive channel of manifestation.

The key to the whole problem lies in this, the life force flows to the point of interest. If the interest and attention are centred upon physical sensation, then the life force will flow, or attempt to flow, through the channel of the reproductive organs, or if denied manifestation, will keep up a constant irritation and stimulation; but if the interest be shifted to an emotional or mental level, then the life force will find an outlet in creative activity upon these levels and drain the pressure from the physical.

The mental and physical habits of a lifetime are not easily broken, but if the thoughts be patiently and persistently kept away from physical sensation and concentrated upon external interests, the law of mental and physical habit will come to our aid, and the life force will learn to flow through its new channel with safety to the individual and benefit to society.

The process of thought control must not be confused with the dissociation of ideas. In dissociation we are dishonest with ourselves, denying that certain qualities exist in our natures; the ideas connected with them are repressed into our subconsciousness, and it is the involuntary subconscious censor that holds them down; whereas in thought control we admit the primitive side of our natures and set to work to train it, and because we know that dwelling upon mental pictures of a sexual nature produces a physical reaction, we exclude these ideas from consciousness; but in this case the repression is not into the subconscious mind, but into the foreconscious, and it is one of the voluntary censors that enforces the command and remains under our control.

The distinction between repression and dissociation must be clearly borne in mind in all re-educational work. A certain amount of repression is unavoidable in a social life; for each individual sacrifices something of his personal desires for the sake of the benefits of cooperation with his fellows, and the energy thus sacrificed is turned to social purposes. Dissociation, however, is always a pathology, and should never be allowed to occur.

14
MALADAPTATION TO ENVIRONMENT AND PSYCHOPATHOLOGY

The classification of diseases was carried out at a time when the body was regarded as the whole of man and the mind looked upon as an unimportant by-product whose influence was negligible. Modern discovery, however, has radically changed our outlook.

Much mental disease has a physical origin and should not be classified as mental at all. To this class belong the mental disturbances arising from disease of or injury to the brain; womb trouble; poisoned blood conditions and the faulty functioning of the ductless glands, whose place in our economy is so important and so little understood; and many other causes of a like nature.

Setting aside this type of disease, with which psychology, strictly speaking, is not concerned, we find the true mental diseases fall into a first broad division, those which are congenital and those which are acquired. In congenital disease an abnormal individual breaks down in a normal environment, and in acquired disease a normal individual breaks down in an abnormal environment. In both cases the results are the same, but treatment and prospect of recovery are very different.

The boundary line between a healthy and diseased mind is not easy to draw, but we may reason a mind diseased when it fails to react normally to its environment; thus, if happenings which should stir us deeply leave us unmoved, or we are upset by things which should have no power to disturb us, we may consider our mind is not working well. Let it never be forgotten, however, that mental disturbance ranges from irritability, depression, and bad memory, to its extreme manifestations in the different forms of insanity.

The division between nervous and mental disease is even harder to draw, but for all practical purposes the sense of reality may be utilised as a dividing line; as soon as he loses his sense of reality a man passes the boundary line of insanity. The neurotic knows that there is something wrong with him, but that the world is all right; the lunatic believes that he is all right, but that there is something wrong with the world.

It is the constant aim of the mind to maintain harmonious relations between the individual and the environment; to secure an adjustment to, and to make the best of, the constantly varying conditions to which the organism is subjected. If it fails to do this, the law of the survival of the fittest comes into action and automatically eliminates the unfit - those who have failed to adapt themselves to the conditions in which they live. Failure to adapt may be due to one of two causes: the individual may be abnormal, or the environment may be abnormal.

Modern social conditions in a civilised community tend to prevent the automatic elimination of the unfit and to permit them to live on. With physical failure to adapt, due to malformation or lack of stamina, we will not deal here, but will confine ourselves to the problem of adjustment on the mental level.

If there is difficulty in making a mental adjustment to environment and finding contentment and peace of mind, then the individual is faced by a peculiar problem, he is allowed to continue his physical life, but cannot find mental peace. In order to obtain relief from this intolerable condition, certain devices are unconsciously resorted to. These devices are of the nature of buffers or shock absorbers, and provided the individual does not deviate too much from the normal type, which is adapted to the environment, and that the environment likewise does not differ too much from the type for which the individual was designed, then these devices effectually protect his feelings from the rude shocks of circumstances and enable him to keep his poise and peace of mind.

If, however, the strain thrown upon the psychic shock absorber is too great for it adequately to absorb, then the rebound of the buffer-springs throws the machinery of the mind out of gear and makes itself felt in nervous and mental disorders. Like physical disease, mental disease is Nature's effort at repair which overreaches itself.

This, then, is what constitutes mental disease (the organic insanities being excluded from this definition) - the reaction of the mind to what it cannot assimilate. It must not be thought, however, that mental disorder necessarily means insanity. Any faulty functioning of the mind comes under the heading of psycho-pathology, and just as the diseases of the body range from a passing indisposition to some fatal organic disease, so the diseases of the mind range from irritability and forgetfulness to the complete collapse of lunacy.

15
CONFLICT

As we have already seen, our life is motived by three great instincts. A moment's thought, however, will cause us to realise that, as these instincts are diverse in their aims, they may sometimes find themselves in opposition to one another; this condition is known to psychologists as CONFLICT, wherein one instinct can only be gratified at the expense of another. For instance, a man may be starving, and be tempted to steal in order to satisfy his hunger. Here we see a conflict between the self-preservation and herd instinct, for if he steals, he may lose his place in the herd, and if he does not steal, he may lose his life, and it is astonishing how many will choose the latter alternative, proving the power and fundamental nature of the herd instinct. The man will be torn two ways, and can only gratify one instinct at the expense of the other. Or, again, he may fall in love with a woman who is denied to him by the marriage laws of his country. Here we see a conflict between the sex instinct and the herd instinct. Or he may fall in love with one whom it would be disadvantageous socially or professionally for him to marry, and here we see a conflict between the sex and self-preservation instincts.

Now, in each of these cases a large amount of force is locked up and rendered unavailable for the general purposes of the life, for a head-on collision between instincts is involved, and each employs the whole of its energy to neutralise the force of the other, and the whole life comes to a standstill while the battle is fought out. It is notorious that an individual in such a dilemma can come to no decision, take no decisive action, in any department of his life. Some solution has to be arrived at, and any solution is better than a continuation of the conflict, the pain of which is intolerable.

First, the man may think the whole matter out, and, acting according to his nature, give the victory to one or other of the combatants, leaving the vanquished instinct to seek adjustment as best it may. It requires great strength, however, to take such a stand, and many are not able to do it. Some seek a solution of the problem by keeping the instincts in separate compartments of the mind, and never comparing their special pleadings, as did a science teacher known to the writer, who on weekdays taught the doctrines of evolution, and on Sundays the doctrine of special creation, and when questioned on the matter, burst into a towering passion and refused to discuss it.

A third solution, however, is very often found by the perplexed mind, and that is known as dissociation.

Now, REPRESSION and DISSOCIATION are two terms current in modern psychological parlance, and the writer has often heard them used as if they were interchangeable terms, but this is not the case. Repression means that certain ideas are put into the subconscious mind and not permitted to return to consciousness, but dissociation means that some of these ideas, instead of lying quiet in the subconscious, split off from the integration of the personality and function independently. These two factors of mentation will be studied in detail in the following chapters.

16
REPRESSION

Repression is a refusal to permit an idea to enter consciousness. The instant it looms up upon the fringe of consciousness the attention is resolutely turned away from it. This device is resorted to when an idea enters the mind which is repugnant to our character, when we find ourselves thinking thoughts which are out of harmony with the general tone of our nature. Unwilling to admit to ourselves that we have such a side to our dispositions, we turn away from the repulsive images; but as it is impossible to erase from the mind any idea which has once entered it, we endeavour to store these ideas, since they must be stored somewhere, in that part which is furthest away from consciousness, and so, to use the technicalities of the psychologist, we repress them into our subconscious.

When it is remembered that every child is born into the world a little savage, and that it is only by education he achieves civilisation, it will readily be seen that our primitive nature is not a thing which our cultivated self can regard with any complacency. That the untrained child is selfish and dirty, we are all aware; and that we ourselves, before our training had time to take effect on us, were also selfish and dirty, we cannot with logic deny; but a merciful veil of forgetfulness has been drawn across this period, for we have developed into something so different from what we were, that our primitive self is utterly repugnant to us, and repression is resorted to to prevent this unpleasant ghost of our original natures from intruding upon our self-esteem.

All ideas of an uncivilised type which enter the mind are apt to call forth a certain amount of response from us - hence the success of the smutty story - for the primitive side of our natures is not dead, and stirs in its sleep if a note of the same pitch is sounded in its hearing; therefore ideas which wake our lower nature are quickly repressed into the subconscious lest they should be translated into action. Repression is essentially the mechanism of self-disgust.

It is still an open question whether repression is normal or abnormal; whether it is part of the functioning of the healthy mind, or whether it is to be regarded as a psychic corn or callosity, an endeavour on the part of nature to reinforce a point of pressure, which, though intended as a defence, is apt to become a disease.

The part played by consciousness in repression is equally an open question. In my opinion, an idea must be present to consciousness before its nature can be apprehended and the judgment formed which leads to its banishment.

There is no question but that, if we were strong enough, we could deal with these problems in the conscious mind by means of thought control, and that repression is only resorted to when the first line of defence has gone down before the onslaught of the lower side of our natures. Repression may therefore be looked upon as a reaction due to weakness; the mind that was perfectly adapted to its environment would assimilate all experiences and grow stronger in the process.

17
DISSOCIATION

While the device of repression may adequately deal with many of the unwelcome thoughts that intrude themselves upon us, it is not capable of doing so in every case, and then the process is carried a stage further, and DISSOCIATION takes place.

Dissociation is pathological forgetting. Emotion is the life of an idea. In ordinary forgetting a memory sinks into the subconscious because insufficient interest is attached to it to enable it to remain in consciousness; if, however, an idea associated with some strong emotion is repressed into the subconscious, that emotion will, as it were, vivify it, and cause it to have an independent life of its own; it splits off from the personality and is said to be dissociated.

It will be noted that in our study of memory we saw that ideas never remain solitary, but its chains of associations manage to evade the censor and ramify through the other levels of the mind with far-reaching consequences, giving rise to much of the illogicality and unreasonableness which disturb our attempts at rational thinking.

We have already noted that a complex is a group of ideas held together by some emotionally toned interest; and as all emotion has its root in an instinct, it follows that all complexes must be affiliated to one or other of the instincts; as they sink into the subconscious they therefore go down the channel of the instinct to which they belong, and as they are swimming against the current they tend to block the flow of that particular instinct and to cause it to express itself through the subsidiary channel which they are endeavouring to open up.

It can readily be seen that serious consequences must arise from an obstacle lodged in the fairway of so great a force and drawing to itself, under the law of association of ideas, all thoughts that may enter the mind on the same subject, or that have a real or symbolic resemblance to it. As has been truly said, the subconscious grows at the expense of the conscious, and the balance of the mind is upset; the thrust of life, the source of all energy, instead of flowing freely from level to level, is blocked by the complex and held up in the subconscious, causing the pressure on that level to rise to danger-point, while the conscious mind is sapped of its vitality, producing an individual of imperative and chaotic needs, which he is unable to formulate, even to himself, and with no power to give them expression or obtain their satisfaction.

18
SYMBOLISATION

We may picture the dissociated complex, with the pressure of an instinct behind it, constantly seeking to evade the censor and return to consciousness, where its wishes can be translated into action; and see how the censor, reinforced by the whole weight of the character, resolutely refuses to permit its escape.

We have seen that the dissociated complex, following the ordinary laws of association, forms alliances with ideas which have a symbolical or fanciful connection with itself. These ideas, not being in themselves objectionable to the character, are permitted by the censor to enter consciousness; then the dissociated complex, taking advantage of its alliance with them, pours its bottled-up emotion along the association-channels thus formed, and so obtained an outlet into consciousness, giving rise, however, to very different results from those which were its original intention, and producing those irrational likes, dislikes, and eccentricities which are characteristic of the person whose mind is not working smoothly.

An example of this is shown in the case of a woman who noticed that the brass plates on doctors' doors had a peculiar fascination for her; when enquiry was made into her story, it was found that, in her youth, she had fallen in love with the family physician, who was a married man; feeling this affection to be wrong, she had firmly put it out of her life (i.e. put it into her subconscious). The association between the doctor and the brass plate was obvious enough, but as brass plates were unobjectionable, the censor offered no resistance to them, and the emotion which centred round the doctor whose image was buried in her subconscious was permitted to reach consciousness transferred to the innocent brass plate.

The subconscious makes use of symbolism in precisely the same way that the poet does, but it employs a device which the poet does not, it remembers that a pair of opposites have a connecting link in their very polarity, and uses a negative to express a positive, if the positive is repugnant to the character. Thus an unmarried woman, whose healthy sex instinct has been denied fulfilment through husband and children, may become morbid, and read literature concerning the repression of the White Slave traffic ad nauseam; and becoming worse, may develop what is called old maids' insanity, and imagine that perfectly innocent men are pestering her with immoral attentions (which in her heart she secretly desires), and go to the police for protection.

19
PHANTASIES, DREAMS, AND DELUSIONS

We have already seen that emotion is intimately allied with instinct, and that it is the thrust of the urging instincts that drives us to action, making us seek to appease the needs of our nature and incidentally fulfil certain racial and evolutionary ends.

Our first attempt, urged on by these promptings, is to bring about the realisation of our desires in the external world by means of bodily effort; but should this effort fail to achieve its purpose, or should circumstances deny us the opportunity to make this effort with any hope of success, then the mind often falls back upon a secondary achievement, and images its success in the realms of phantasy and make-believe, where there are no laws of cause and effect to check its operations, and Cinderella in her kitchen constructs a phantasy of the Prince's ball. She sees her wish acted out to its fulfilment in the theatre of her mind.

This factor in our nature influences a large proportion of our mental processes, and is considered to be the chief factor in determining the nature, not only of our dreams, but also of the symptoms of nervous and mental diseases, as will be seen later.

During sleep the avenues of the physical senses, whereby impressions reach the mind, are more or less closed, and the ego, which never ceases its activities, is thrown back upon the resources of its memories. Unguided by the reason and judgment, it reviews these, following along the chains of associated ideas according to the laws of memory, which we considered in an earlier chapter.

These wanderings, however, though carried out with the

illogicality which distinguishes the lower levels of our mind, are not entirely purposeless, being determined by various factors. It may be that physical or sensory impressions, dimly discerned during sleep through the partially closed doors of the senses, will give rise to a train of thought, or the matters upon which the mind has been busied during the day may continue to occupy it in an undirected fashion during sleep; but the dream-determining element to which most attention has been directed in modern psychology is the upsurging of the instinctive wishes which have been denied fulfilment in waking life, so that in our dreams we see realised, as in phantasy, the wishes which have failed to gain realisation in reality, or may even have failed to gain access to our consciousness owing to the operation of the censor which strives to exclude from consciousness all distressing or repulsive matters; for in sleep all our painfully acquired civilisation falls away from us, the higher centres of our being are in abeyance, and our primitive, natural self, controlled but never abolished, expresses its fundamental, untutored desires in their elemental form.

These wishes, however, are seldom expressed directly. So foreign are they to our civilised selves that even in sleep our habits of thinking assert themselves and exercise some check upon what shall be expressed; but they are generally distorted almost beyond recognition by the substitutions of more acceptable ideas for crude images of instinctive needs, and as the subconscious mind links ideas together according to their superficial or accidental associations, it will be seen that strange and tangled dramas will be acted out upon the stage of the mind in an effort to represent the fulfilment of some primitive instinctive wish.

Modern methods of psychological research make much use of dreams in the effort to investigate the levels of the mind to which we have no direct access, and psychotherapy uses the same method in order to trace the disorders of the mind to their cause. For if the train of thought which the mind has followed in its progression from a crude instinctive, often physical, wish to the completed dream-drama be traced back again from the images of the dream to the underlying ideas which gave rise to them, we can lay bare the hidden springs of motive and character; hence the great use that has been made of the method of dream analysis in modern psychotherapy.

It is interesting to note that the delusions of lunatics are constructed upon exactly the same principles as the phantasies of our castles in the air; they also represent the fulfilment of wishes that have been denied their realisation, and have achieved their ultimate form through the same primitive methods of thinking that are responsible for our dreams; in fact, they may be looked upon as a phantasy which has progressed a step nearer realisation than the day-dream.

The symptoms of the hysteric have a similar origin, but represent the wishes of dissociated complexes instead of the wishes of the whole personality as happens in insanity.

Thus we may see that, should our desires be denied expression in our lives, they will construct dream castles for themselves during sleep in which we may temporarily dwell as monarch of all we survey; and should these desires be very imperative, should a large part of our nature be involved in them, then the dream may overflow into waking consciousness, and we shall live among our own subjective mind pictures, instead of among objective realities, and act out the part we have assigned ourselves in the dream drama, to the consternation of onlookers who pronounce us insane.

The lunatic, however, is not irrational, he is absolutely rational if once his premises be granted, for he carries the logical deductions from these premises to their ultimate conclusion. And once it be realised that some fundamental and essentially natural wish lies at the root of these phantasies which we see him acting out, then we shall see that the clue to the treatment of insanity lies in these wishes and the region of the mind that gives rise to them.

20
PSYCHOTHERAPY

While many forms of mental disease have a physical origin in the brain, nervous systems and state of the blood, many others are purely mental from beginning to end, although the body may be chosen as the scene of some of their manifestations. Modern medicine is learning to deal with mental diseases by mental methods, and of these the principal types maybe of interest. It must be remembered, however, that psychotherapy is the youngest of the sciences, and is still in its experimental stage; and that though magnificent work has been done by the pioneers, they cannot claim to have said the last word upon the structure of the human mind, for even if they knew all that was to be known, leaving nothing to be discovered by future investigation, which they would be the last to claim on their own behalf, though their disciples are not always blessed with the same modesty of genius, evolution is moving on, with the human mind at its apex, so that statements which were true of human nature before the Great War may have to be modified when the Great Peace becomes an established fact.

Our knowledge of the mind, its diseases and therapy, is far from complete. The investigation of each human mind is in the nature of a voyage of discovery; though the coastline of the mental landscape may be known to us, the hinterland is unmapped. We do not know what lies behind the human personality; we are equally ignorant of the exact nature of its relations with its environment, and while our knowledge is in this state we cannot speak upon any point with finality.

21
PSYCHOANALYSIS

The foundations of this method and theory were laid by Sigmund Freud of Vienna, and set forth by him in his epoch-making book, the Interpretation of Dreams, published in 1900. Two schools of psychoanalysis exist at the present time: the Vienna school, which adheres strictly to the doctrines of Freud; and the Zurich school, which subscribes to a modification of these doctrines as taught by Dr.Jung.

While both schools agree upon general principles and as to the anatomy of the mind, they differ in their teaching as to the modus operandi of mental disease. Freud holds that functional nervous disorders are due to the retention by the subconscious mind of an infantile attitude towards life, and especially towards sex, and that this attitude, which should have been outgrown and left behind, sets up stresses and strains in the mind which lead to the manifestations of mental disease. He gives us the concept of the accumulation of emotion in this wound in the mind, just as pus accumulates in an abscess, giving rise to tenderness and pain. He conceives the function of the psychoanalyst to be to lance this abscess by bringing the subject of distress into consciousness, whereby the repressed emotion is realised and fully experienced, and thereby got rid of. This process is technically known as ABREACTION.

The psychologist who conducts the analysis is very likely to be the recipient of this repressed emotion because, at the moment of its arrival in consciousness, he is apt to be standing in the line of fire. This acceptance of the repressed emotion by the operator is conceived to be a most important phase of the cure, and is known as the TRANSFERENCE.

That this factor of the transference opens a door to most serious difficulties and dangers cannot be denied. The via media between undue influence and callous indifference is hard to find. It is maintained that more analysis will work off the emotion which much analysis has succeeded in lying bare, but in actual practice the process is not so simple and often leads to complications.

This transference of emotion to the analyst, together with the deleterious effects of continual and prolonged dwelling upon the unsavoury aspects of life which takes place in a psycho-analysis, constitute serious objections to this method of therapy.

Jung holds that mental disease is due to a failure of adaptation in the present, leading to regression to an infantile mode of thinking. It will thus be seen that the two theories, while based upon the same data, are fundamentally different, and must lead to differences in practical application.

Both schools explore the subconscious mind by means of dream analysis, and to this method the Zurich school also adds the method known as word reaction. The process of dream analysis is extremely complicated. Briefly, the patient is instructed to recount a dream, and this dream is then taken point by point, and the 'free associations' traced out in the following manner. He is instructed to take an image in his dream as a starting-point, turn his mind loose, and watch where it goes, the theory being that it will retrace the association train of ideas by which the dream image was derived from the underlying wish. An elaborate technique exists for interpreting these dream images; so elaborate as to be beyond the scope of the present volume.

How much of this technique is sound and how much is arbitrary is still a matter of opinion among psychologists; we have little data as yet as to the part played by unintentional suggestion on the part of the psychoanalyst, no doubt a considerable factor in some cases, and an exceedingly falsifying and misleading one.

The word association method of Jung is less open to objection on the ground of arbitrariness, and its operation is simpler. A list of anything from a dozen to a hundred or more words is made out. The first half-dozen words have usually no particular significance, but then follow a series of words believed to be specially associated with the different types of complex which may become split off from consciousness; lists of these have been worked out by different students of this school, but although one of these lists is usually used as a basis, the analyst generally inserts words which he believes will especially bear upon the patient's particular problems. These words are called out to the patient, one at a time, and he is instructed to utter the first word that comes into his head in connection with each. The time he takes to do this is taken by a stop-watch usually working to one-fifth of a second. The first half-dozen of unimportant words will show the patient's average reaction time, but if any words among the subsequent ones have special significance for him, there will be a perceptible lengthening of the time he takes to reply; moreover the replies may be curious, and either show special bearing upon his problems, or, by their irrelevancy, show that the original idea was discarded as unspeakable and a substitute hastily extemporised. If the list be read over again it will be found that, whereas those words which have no special significance are usually responded to by the same reaction word, those which bear upon the patient's emotions produce a change in the reaction word. Free association is then resorted to, as in the case of dream symbols, to discover the underlying train of ideas and the factors in the subconscious from which they derive their emotion.

Many Freudians make use of this method also, and indeed the two methods of dream analysis and word association are generally regarded as supplementary. The chief value of the latter lies in the fact that it can be used in cases where the patient is either unable or reluctant to co-operate.

The difference in the view-point of the two schools of psychoanalysis leads to a difference in the method of handling the patient; the Freudian who believes that all nerve trouble is due to the retention of infantile habits of thinking, confines himself to analysis and nothing but analysis, offering the patient little or nothing in the way of explanation or instruction, but simply aiding him to lay bare the depths of his subconscious mind, believing that by so doing pent-up emotions will be worked off and split-off complexes reassociated to the personality. The disciple of Jung, on the other hand, believing that the trouble is due to a present failure of adaptation, though using the psychoanalytic method to reveal and bring into consciousness the dissociated complexes, uses a considerable amount of teaching and explanation in an endeavour to enable the patient to assimilate the fruits of experience and adapt himself to his environment. The Freudian complains that the follower of Jung beclouds the issue by unintentional suggestion, and the latter accuses the former of unnecessarily prolonging the process by leaving the patient to find his own way unaided by a wider experience.

The teaching and explanatory method, generally known as re-education, is chiefly associated with the name of du Bois, who was its original exponent, but as, in his day, the psychoanalytic method of investigating the causes of mental disease was unknown, he was often groping in the dark, and dealing with secondary symptoms and effects, so that his method fell into disrepute in the eyes of the new school; but that this method, wisely handled, can be of great benefit in expediting a cure and lessening the painfulness of the process is beyond gainsay.

22
HYPNOSIS, SUGGESTION, AND AUTOSUGGESTION

Much popular misapprehension exists with regard to the phenomenon known as hypnosis. It may briefly be described as a condition in which the reason and judgment of the subject are in temporary abeyance, and any idea presented to him will be accepted without reflection, and take so strong a hold upon the mind that it will act itself out almost automatically. This condition of passive receptivity graduates from slight abstraction, almost undistinguishable from normal consciousness to a condition resembling sleep, or the cataleptic rigidity of deep trance. Its manifestations and characteristics are manifold and most furious and instructive, but beyond the scope of the present work.

Different hypnotists use different methods of inducing this condition, but the main factor in all of them is the fixation and arrestation of the attention and the use of suggestion. It is generally held that it is autosuggestion on the part of the subject, induced by the hypnotist, that is the crux of the whole problem, and that without this internal cooperation, which is often of an unconscious and involuntary nature, the work of the operator would be unavailing.

Hypnosis is the oldest known method of psychotherapy, and, in conjunction with psycho-analysis, is coming to the front again in the treatment of nervous cases and especially of shell shock.

The term suggestion is apt to be used somewhat loosely to denote any concept offered by one person to another, but in its psychological sense it is used to denote those ideas which are slipped into the mind of a person without being submitted to his judgment; in its psychotherapeutic sense, however, it is reserved for the process of inserting ideas in the mind while the patient is in a state of artificially induced drowsiness, but not unconscious under deep hypnosis.

Autosuggestion, or the insertion of ideas in the subconscious by the conscious mind of the person concerned, has been reduced to a therapeutic system by the New Nancy School of psychology, and is associated with the name of Emile Coue. It is held by this school that suggestibility, or the faculty of permitting ideas to so possess the mind that they express themselves in action, is a normal human faculty; and although it is the cause of many, or even most of the ills that both mind and body are heir to, it is not in itself a morbid condition, but is a necessary factor, in educability, evil only arising when wrong ideas exploit this faculty. We can, however, equally well make use of it for the expression of good ideas, with great benefit to our character and health. Suggestion, and, in intractable cases, hypnosis, is made use of by the New Nancy School, not as a direct remedial method but to teach the use of autosuggestion whereby the patient cures himself and is able to prevent any recrudescence of his malady. It is claimed that this method increases a person's self-reliance instead of undermining it, and is of the greatest value, not only as a therapeutic agent, but as an educational method, and its use in this aspect is urged. But although it is of acknowledged value in the cure of disease, it is questionable whether it might not lead to artificiality and warping of the nature if applied to the growing mind that was developing along normal lines. Only the most judicious guidance could avoid this pitfall.

It is impossible in a book of this nature to give a knowledge of the psychotherapeutic methods that can be of any practical use; the reader must refer to the many text-books upon the subject if such is desired. It must, however, be realised that the modern methods of dealing with the mind are extremely potent, and that it is possible to completely wreck a nature by their injudicious use. A knowledge, however, of the principles of mental hygiene can be nothing but beneficial, though the actual treatment of mental or nervous disease should be avoided by the amateur, for, whatever his theoretical knowledge, work can alone give accuracy of diagnosis. The beginnings of certain forms of insanity are very hard to distinguish from nerve trouble, even by the expert and the amateur who tries his prentice hand upon such a case by mistake is likely to have his error painfully and forcibly impressed upon his mind.

Psychotherapy is the youngest of the sciences and in a state of vigorous and healthy growth, but there is as yet no orthodox body of doctrine which is regarded as being thoroughly established and accepted by all schools of thought. The lay reader, for whom this book is designed, would do well to be on his guard against dogmatic expressions of opinion which may be presented to him, either in lecture or in print, for our knowledge is not in a state to warrant them. We have learnt much, but we do not know all, and until we know much more than we do now, we must keep an open mind and judge tentatively. The popular vogue of applied psychology among those who are not in a position to form first-hand opinions makes this warning necessary. There is no 'truth once and for all delivered' by a prophet on a mountain, but an earnest band of men and women adding stone by stone to the temple of human knowledge.

The various methods of psychotherapy outlined here have each and all their value, but no one of them is a panacea for all the ills that flesh is heir to; the science is in its infancy, and the percentage of cure is by no means satisfactory.

There is no standard of training for either medical men or lay analysts, and owing to the great emphasis laid upon sex by the modern schools, the method is open to grave abuses in inexpert or unclean hands.

23
THE PRACTICAL APPLICATION
OF PSYCHOLOGY

Those who have read the foregoing pages will see that there are certain broad divisions into which they fall. Let us now review these divisions in their relation to the practical art of living.

The first great division we studied was concerned with the levels into which the mind was divided and the types of thinking which were carried on in each of them. The problems of memory and concentration are closely concerned with these levels and the interrelations between them. If an idea, after entering the mind, disappears into the subconscious, we say it is forgotten and regard it as lost. This, we have seen, is not the case, however. It is stored in the subconscious, and we can make use of it even if we cannot gain direct access to it.

There is an old story concerning the advice that was given to a judge newly raised to the bench, 'Give your decision, it is probably right; but do not give your reasons, the are very likely to be wrong'. Which is merely a pithy way of saying: 'Let your subconscious work out your decision in the light of the enormous masses of data it possesses, including the exact reproduction of every law-book you have ever read, every remark, however casual, you have ever heard, together with the accumulated experience of your race, all of which you are heir to, and it will probably be right; but if you try to rationalise this decision, to explain it in terms of your conscious knowledge, you may make mistakes, because your conscious mind does not know nearly as much as your subconscious.'
If we would learn to trust our subconscious methods of thinking, we should be astonished to find what they are capable of. Genius might be defined as the power of utilising the subconscious mind, and inspiration as a subliminal uprush.

Memory also can be greatly improved by taking advantage of the faculty of association of ideas, a faculty upon which the different memory systems are founded. If we take any idea we wish to remember and clearly image it in association with some idea of the same class that is so familiar to us that it is a permanent part of our mental furniture, then the two concepts will get stuck together, and we can always use the second to summon the first.

The instincts and their development and method of functioning form a second great division of our subject. It will be seen that we must view our life in relation to the instincts and not to the reason, but it must not be forgotten that the instincts themselves are evolving or rather perhaps becoming modified in their expressions by the pressure of new conditions, and in the course of their evolution are being steadily socialised and civilised, so although we must realise that, in their primitive form, they lie at the base of our being, yet in their evolved form they also function at its apex, and that if we are to live well, we must harmonise their manifestation upon every level of our being. The third and most important division, from the standpoint of practical living, is that which deals with the mechanisms by means of which the mind adapts itself to its environment. We should make it our aim to achieve adaptation in the conscious mind by absorbing and assimilating all experience, realising that we can learn our lessons from that which is evil as well as from that which is good, and that any experience, however evil, from which we learn a lesson is converted from poison into food.

While it is necessary that certain types of ideas should be repressed lest they should translate themselves into action, let us never forget that repression need not necessarily imply dissociation, which is an unmixed evil. Dissociation would never occur if we were honest with ourselves. When we refuse to admit, even to ourselves, that our nature possesses certain primitive aspects, we prevent the ideas connected with these aspects from being affiliated to our personality and taking their place in our mental life; they therefore become foreign bodies in the mind, technically termed dissociated complexes, which function independently of the main ego complex.

Instead of taking this attitude, let us recognise the existence of these primitive impulses in ourselves; and when we find their manifestations obtruding themselves, let us gently but firmly put them in their place, and see to it that they do not obtain the upper hand.

Let us never forget the enormous power of auto-suggestion, for the subconscious mind will tend to translate into action any image that is presented to it sufficiently vividly, especially if that image be charged with emotion. Let us therefore be very careful what mental pictures we permit ourselves to dwell upon persistently, whether with fear or desire, for they will mould our lives and even our circumstances to an extent we little realise.

Our whole aim should be to maintain the integrity of the personality, to prevent any splitting off of complexes of ideas, and to see that the instincts, welling up in the deeper levels of our nature, should find their channels clear and unobstructed, so that they may flow out into action on the higher levels of our life.

24
CONCLUSION

It has been said that there is no scrap of knowledge concerning the remotest star which will not, sooner or later, be found to have its bearing upon the problems of human life, and we may well ask what the science of human nature itself has to contribute to the solution of our daffy problems.

The practical application of psychology has certain well-defined spheres. Its bearing upon education has long been recognised, and much valuable work done in relation to the study of the child mind. The psychology of fatigue, in relation to industrial efficiency, has also found recognition as a branch of applied science not without its practical value. The field of social problems is still largely awaiting exploration, and there can be little doubt that the study of the psychology of the criminal and unemployable would yield results of the greatest social value.

At the present moment, it is the field of abnormal psychology that holds the focus of attention. That inestimably valuable results are being obtained in this field of study no one can dispute, but its value is not confined to the relief of disease alone, but, as the research is progressing deeper, to the revelation of the conditions that give rise to disease. Just as the study of pathology gave us the science of hygiene, so the study of mental diseases is showing us the way to healthier thinking. It is teaching us that any abnormal attitude towards life will produce mental discomfort, if not actual disease, and it is showing us, just as physiological hygiene has shown us, that if the developing intelligence of man leads him to depart from primitive conditions wherein the instincts are sufficient guides, then he must also apply his reason to the new problems to which the new conditions give rise, and not leave the solution of these to instincts which are only fitted for the simplest form of functioning. The instinct of combativeness, or the instinct of flight, will not conduct the evolutions of a modern army, and neither will the primitive impulses enable man to live well and happily in conditions which elaborate mental processes have built up - as witness the terrible prevalence of unsolved sex problems beneath the fair show of our civilisation. Two-thirds, if not more, of nerve trouble have their origin in the efforts of a primitive instinct to function under civilised conditions and its failure to make the adaptation. We need to take our instincts out of the region of the subconscious and apply our reason to them if we are to solve the problems that press upon us.

Throughout this book it will have been seen that stress has been laid upon the functioning and activity of those levels of the mind that are below the threshold of consciousness, and that it has been pointed out that the instincts, and not the reason, are the key to the human mind. But it has also been shown that the mind is in a state of evolution, and that reason, as its latest development, has an equal biological significance with the instincts of sex and self-preservation, and that we can no more afford to ignore the higher attributes of the human mind than we can afford to deny their true place to the primitive.

Briefly, the primitive man lies at the base of our being, but the divine man stands at its apex, and we, in our ascent, are in a transition stage, with subconscious and superconscious not yet correlated in the conscious mind. We do not see our past and future save in the dim pictures of dream and vision, by the uncertain gleam of intuition rather than the clear light of reason, and no solution of any human problem, either social or psychological, can be valid which does not look to the future as well as the past. Hitherto psychology has sought its standards of normality in the primitive and subhuman, forgetting that the flower of humanity is a natural product as well as its weeds; that religion, charity and idealism are as much a part of human nature as those primitive instincts which give rise to unnameable crimes. A psychology which looks to the past can show us causes, but it is only a psychology which looks to the future which can find us cures. Evolution did not cease its progress when it produced the cave man guarding his family, but evolved the 'Save the Children Fund', which before the echoes of the last shot had died away was sending succour to the helpless young of an enemy herd.

A psychology which bases its philosophy upon a return to the primitive, especially if that psychology undertakes the solution of human problems, individual or collective, is ignoring the data of evolution. We know that all life originated in the sea, and that the young of many species still pass the first phase of their life in the water. When, however, they have come ashore, and the gills have given place to lungs, they cease to be water creatures, and the structural traces of their origin are vestigial and not functional, and a frog can be drowned as easily as any other air-breathing creature, despite his tadpole past. So it is with the human psyche, unquestionably it has passed through a primitive phase in the course of its development, but if, in an effort to remedy some faulty development, it be thrust back to that phase after evolving to a higher one, it will perish as surely as the frog thrust under water. It should be the aim of psychotherapy, not to reduce the mind to its primitive elements and point of view, but rather to help humanity to make that transition from the lower to the higher which evolution is forcing upon us, whether we will or no. Adaptation to environment is the key to life, and the environment to which an individual must be aided to adjust himself, if such aid be sought, is not that environment which, generation by generation, is receding further into the past, but that future which hour by hour is becoming the present, and from which there is no escape.

It should be the aim of psychotherapy to work out the arc which evolution is describing, and to set the feet of racial wanderers upon its path. It is a futile and dangerous philosophy which proposes a return to the past as an escape from the present.

Geology, zoology, sociology, and comparative psychology, all show us the evolution of that which is simple into that which is complex, from the cave man, with his few needs and problems, to the complications of a modern industrial society. And we see in the little segment of the evolutionary arc with which we are most closely concerned that the chief factor is the herd instinct which is pressing us all the time towards a more complete socialisation of humanity, and that any adaptation which an individual makes must be in relation to his integration as a social unit and not to his needs as a solitary individual.

Diagnostic and descriptive psychology must be distinguished from remedial psychology of which we have had all too little. Research on the abnormal mind alone will not give us the key to a healthy life, we must study social psychology as well as individual psychology, because man is a social animal, and his mental processes are determined by this fact; any adaptation he makes, and adaptation is the basis of psychotherapy, must be in relation to his social group as well as to his own subconscious wishes; it is not enough to bring these wishes into the light of consciousness, they must be synthesised with the rest of the personality, to the social organisation of which that personality is a unit, and to the great evolutionary drift of which even the race itself is but a partial expression. Psychotherapy may begin with the primitive, but it must end with the divine, for both are integral factors in the human mind.

BIBLIOGRAPHY

Whosoever desires to penetrate deeper into the study of psychology will find an immense mass of literature awaiting his consideration. I say consideration advisedly, because the lay student cannot realise too clearly that, despite whatever leaders or followers of the different schools of thought may say, there is no accepted criterion of psychological doctrine. There is much carefully recorded data available for his study, and all shades of opinion for his acceptance, but no standard authority to whom he can refer, and the writer, even in the course of her own studies in this subject, has seen orthodox opinion shift its ground too often for her to believe that, even in this department of science, evolution has ceased its work and the millennium set in.

The study of psychology falls into certain broad divisions, though a sound knowledge of the general principles of the science is essential as a basis for any specialised reading; but the student will find the field is so wide that he is compelled to limit his cultivation to a chosen aspect if he is to do more than glean the hedges. Temperament and avocation must determine the choice, but it may be helpful to point out certain landmarks.

William James may be looked upon as the grandfather of psychology, and much of his work, having penetrated to fundamentals, has a quality which renders it classical and makes it the basis of any superstructure which newer schools may raise. His books, though of massive bulk, are delightfully readable, and being of a descriptive and classificatory rather than a theorising nature, form a valuable counterpoise to newer and more daring schools of thought.
The elements from which the mind is built up are admirably defined and dealt with by William James in his standard

work, the Principles of Psychology, and on the basis he laid down has grown up the section of psychology which forms the theoretical basis of the art of teaching.

Another vast and most interesting field of research is that which is opened up by physiological psychology; it might perhaps be contended that this ground truly belongs to physiology rather than to the study of the mind, for its methods are those of the physiological laboratory; but no adequate grasp of the subject is possible without its aid, for it shows us the methods of interaction and mutual influence between mind and body, which, in the opinion of the writer, is one of the vital points in this branch of knowledge. Professor McDougal, in his little book, Physiological Psychology, gives an epitome which could hardly be improved upon for the study of the brain and nervous system from the standpoint of psychology; but there is another unit in the machinery whereby mind expresses itself upon the physical plane, one that is only just beginning to be recognised, and that is the wonderful system of interacting organs known as the endocrine glands, which seems to be the vehicle of the emotions. A very interesting popular epitome of this subject is given by Dr. Berman in his book, The Glands Controlling Personality, but, unfortunately, he gives neither his authorities, nor the data upon which his statements are based, but if this book be read in conjunction with an extraordinarily illuminating piece of work, The Sex Complex, by Dr. Blair Bell, the reader will be able to obtain an adequate grasp of the subject. The Sex Complex only deals with one aspect of the endocrine problem, but being most admirably worked out, enables the principles of glandular polity to be clearly perceived. Neither of these books are written from the psychological standpoint, but if read from that standpoint, throw much light in dark places.

The principal place in modern psychology is occupied by the doctrines of the psycho-analytical school, and no one can be said to have an adequate knowledge of the subject who is not familiar with these doctrines, whether he agrees with all their findings or not. If William James is regarded as the grandfather of modern psychology, then Freud, the founder of this school, must be regarded as its father. The great difficulty which confronts the lay student of this aspect of the science of the mind is the extreme unpleasantness of its subject matter, and the fact that it seems to obsess its devotees till all sense of proportion is lost, and they cease to be scientifically impartial and become gratuitously nasty, and the writer, while acknowledging, as all must, the supreme indebtedness of science to the researches of this school, would warn the lay reader against taking its extremer doctrines too seriously, for, just as the human body contains other organs than those used exclusively for generation and excretion, so the human mind contains ideas besides those relating to these two subjects, and probably, when the last analysis is made (which has not yet been done), the proportion between the two aspects of activity will be found to be the same in both cases.

A grasp of this subject, however, as has been said, is essential for the understanding of modern psychology, and it is presented in admirable form for the layman in The Psychology of Insanity by Bernard Hart, a book which is not nearly so terrible as its title would lead one to believe, and which reveals in a most delightful fashion the workings of human nature, and can provide the astute reader with quite as much amusement at the expense of his friends as any treatise on the art of telling fortunes from teacups. Another book which presents the doctrines of psychoanalysis in a readable manner is Dr. Maurice Nicholls Dream Psychology, which, whether one considers it advisable or not to subject the mind to this method of treatment, shows clearly how it is done. Dr. Paul Bousfield also gives a very clear outline of modern doctrines on this subject.

Suggestion and hypnosis also form part of the modern doctor's stock-in-trade, and their findings throw much light upon psychology in general. Moll's book on hypnotism gives a mass of details which will enable the reader to picture the process to himself and form some concept of its nature, and Dr. William Brown's book, Psychology and Psychotherapy shows its application in the modern methods of treating disease. The fascinating subject of the influence of mind upon body is dealt with in a book which the writer regards as epoch-making, Suggestion and Auto-suggestion by Baudouin, wherein is shown the scientific basis of the empirical methods of M. Coue.

A most interesting school of social psychology is growing up upon the basis laid by Professor McDougal, and his book, An Introduction to Social Psychology, forms an admirable guide to this section of the field; but supreme for its insight and the vistas it opens up, remains, in the writer's opinion, Dr. Trotter's Instincts of the Herd; and no one should study the Freudian psychology without also reading this book which will enable him to see the subject of the instincts in its true proportion.

Finally, for a general text-book upon the subject of modern psychology, which gives an outline of the doctrines of the various schools and shows their relation one to another, the most useful all-round book which we have upon psychology at the present time, and upon which the student can entirely rely for a fair presentation of what has been established and accepted, as distinguished from the hypothetical which awaits proof (a distinction not always made by other writers), the author would recommend The New Psychology and its Relation to Life by Mr. A. G. Tansley, to whom she is indebted for the foreword to this little book.

If the student, having grasped the general outline given in the present pages, will proceed to Mr. Tansley's book and get its subject matter safely stowed away in his head, he can then browse at leisure over the literature of the subject, certain of obtaining that coordination of knowledge without which information is a source of error.

THE SOCIETY OF THE INNER LIGHT

The Society of the Inner Light is a Society for the study of Occultism, Mysticism, and Esoteric Psychology and the development of their practice.

Its aims are Christian and its methods are Western.

Students who, after due inquiry, desire to pursue their studies further, may take the Correspondence Course. Their training will be in the theory of Esoteric Science, and they will be given the discipline which prepares for its practice.

For further details apply for a copy of the WORK & AIMS of the Society from:

> The Secretariat
> The Society of the Inner Light
> 38 Steele's Road
> London NW3 4RG

THE INNER LIGHT JOURNAL, a Quarterly Magazine, founded by Dion Fortune, is devoted to the study of Mysticism, Esoteric Christianity, Occult Science, and the Psychology of Superconsciousness. Annual Subscription £16.00.

It is because my novels are packed with such things as these (symbolism directed to the subconcious) that I want my students to take them seriously. The 'Mystical Qabalah' gives the theory, but the novels give the practice. Those who read the novels without having studied the 'Qabalah' will get hints and a stimulus to their subconcious. Those who study the Qabalah without reading the novels will get an interesting intellectual jig-saw puzzle to play with; but those who study the 'Mystical Qabalah' with the help of the novels get the keys of the Temple put into their hands. As the Lord said: "Know ye not that your body is the temple of the Holy Ghost?"

DION FORTUNE

Dion Fortune's ability as a chronicler of the esoteric can only in the end be equalled by the acknowledged talent of Huysmans and Charles Williams.

THE WINGED BULL   A ROMANCE OF MODERN MAGIC

The message of the book concerns the spiritualising of sex. But not the spiritualising of sex by sublimating it onto other planes than the spiritual, but the spiritualising of sex by realising its profound spiritual significance and far-reaching psychological values.

The relationship between a man and a woman in the light of the forgotten knowledge of the ancients and of the Black Mass - which is an abuse of that knowledge - form the background of the story.

The man whom Ursula Brangwyn loves becomes involved in Black Magic and drags her after him. Her brother, a student of strange arts, knows that the only way he can rescue her is to make her transfer her affections to someone else. He chooses his man and sets to work on his difficult task, making use of certain aspects of the sex relationship that are the carefully guarded secrets of the initiates. The story shows the deliberate building of a curious magnetic rapport between two people who do not attract each other. A highly strung, highly cultured sophisticated girl and an unemployed ex-officer, hard bitten and disillusioned.

THE GOAT FOOT GOD

Desperate and wretched after his wife's death at the hands of her lover, Hugh Paston turns to the Ancient Mysteries in search of Pan to re-establish and confirm his own manhood. With another seeker, Paston acquires an old monastary intending to convert it to a temple of Pan. The building is troubled by the spirit of a fifteenth century prior, walled up for his heretically pagan beliefs, who also searched for the goat-foot God. This entity plans to take over Paston's body to pursue his unremitting quest and it is left to Mona, Paston's partner's niece to help solve the problem of human love in this case, when in reality man and woman become representatives of the God and the Goddess.

The Goat foot God is a further example of Dion Fortune's art and her ability to touch the unconscious with well chosen words in place of the equivocal images of classical alchemy. The attitude of anyone fully absorbing the message latent in The Goat Foot God will be subtly changed for the better by the experience.

'Shoots with remarkable success at a most ambitious target.' – The Guardian

SECRETS OF DR TAVERNER

Just as the orthodox scientist tracks out and defeats the bacteria that poison the physical body, so Dr Taverner the healer of sick souls, has to track out and defeat the dark agents of evil which attack his patients.

Crossing the threshold to other mysterious, unorthodox worlds he employs esoteric technique for diagnosis and cure.

Based on real people, this collection of short stories, presents Dion Fortune's teacher (said to be Dr Moriarty) with herself cast in the role of his assistant, Rhodes. Taverner uses his abilities to cure the severely mentally disturbed by esoteric techniques. By technical work on the inner planes he frees his patients from frustration, misery and worse. Rhodes, though just a learner, becomes more and more engrossed in the work until the day she overreaches herself, just like the Sorcerer's Apprentice; only just escaping terror-drenched disaster.

Each story highlights a psycho-esoteric aspect; vampirism, astral journeying, karmic repercussions, demonic interference; and this edition includes a previously unpublished story.

THE DEMON LOVER

Young and innocent Veronica is taken on as Mr. Lucas' secretary though he has other plans for her... Without fully realising just what is going on Veronica finds herself involved in the work of a mysterious sinister male-only magical Lodge.
In spite of Lucas' ruthless exploitation she falls in love with him and becomes an accessory in his occult workings.

To try to protect her from the wrath of the Lodge because of her unlooked for and unwanted passion, Alec Lucas is immersed deeper and deeper into the darkness of the Underworld, ever struggling to free himself from many hells.

This was Dion Fortune's first novel, based on real characters and experiences. It offers many insights not only into the inner nature of the Mysteries and the dangers of Black Magic but also defines aspects of the sacred nature of love.

When it was published the Times Literary Supplement considered it to be 'exceedingly well-written', and it has stood the test of time.

THE SEA PRIESTESS

In Dion Fortune's own words; "This book stands on its own feet as a literary Melchizedek."

It is a book with an undercurrent; upon the surface a romance; underneath a thesis upon a theme; "All women are Isis and Isis is all women."

Further, it is an experiment in prose rhythms which beat upon the subconscious mind in the same way as the Eastern Mantra, which, because they are archaic, speak to the archaic level of the mind whence dreams arise.

At the time she wrote THE SEA PRIESTESS Dion Fortune considered with good reason, that the psychological state of modern civilisation was hardly much of an improvement on the sanitation of a mediaeval walled city. Therefore she dedicated this work to the great goddess Cloacina, the goddess whose function it was to cleanse the drains of the Ancient Rome.

Wilfred Maxwell, a 'wimp' by any standards learns to assert himself, his creativity and full masculinity under the tutelage of the mysterious Vivien Le Fay Morgan. His asthmatic condition has induced a certain psychism and he has a dream vision at the full moon of his patroness as the High Priestess of the Ancient Moon cult who has returned to calm and control the sea by the house he is now embellishing.

All the above are available from;

> The Secretariat
> The Society of the Inner Light
> 38 Steele's Road
> London NW3 4RG

at £7.00 each paperback, plus postage and packaging. Cash with order. Please make cheques out to SIL TRADING LTD.